Carson City
THE EARLY YEARS

Foreword

The great explorer John C. Fremont and his renowned guide Kit Carson blazed their way through this area on their way to California. In the early 1860s the boom of the Comstock Lode and its vast amounts of silver made Carson City a supply and political center for the Great Basin.

Carson City, which became Nevada's capital in 1864, was also a stop on the Pony Express.

The *Nevada Appeal* has been there pretty much from the beginning. On May 16, 1865, frontier raconteur Henry Rust Mighels was on a stagecoach eastbound for Carson City to take over the editorship of what was then the budding *Morning Appeal*. The coach crashed and Mighels wrote his first story for the Appeal detailing that near-fatal accident.

But it's really the photographs that tell the story of Carson City's beginnings. Thanks to the folks at the Nevada State Museum and Nevada State Railroad Museum, particularly Richard Reitnauer, Kyle Wyatt, and Bob Nylen, curator of history for the museum, we had plenty of photographs to choose from. Bob burned the midnight oil as he gathered all of the caption information for the photographs and for that we are eternally grateful.

Most of the photographs in this book were gleaned from the museum's collections of Daun Bohall, Frances Humphrey, Frank Day, Noreen Humphreys, Adrian Atwater, and Ted Wurm.

We also need to thank Brad Fenison of Pediment Publishing from Portland, Oregon, a former newspaper publisher who brought us an idea and an opportunity to share with you a camera's-eye glimpse of Carson City's early years.

We hope you enjoy this Pictorial History.

Jeff Ackerman
Editor and Publisher of the Nevada Appeal

Early Settlement

When the thundering hordes of Forty-Niners began tromping across the country toward California's gold, western Nevada was a sagebrush wilderness, inhabited mainly by jackrabbits. In fact, it wasn't even Nevada. It was Utah Territory.

An enterprising fellow by the name of Frank Hall put up a trading post along the paths to the gold mines in 1851.

One day Frank Hall shot an eagle with his Colt revolver then hung the eagle skin over the door of the station. The valley in which Carson City is located was named Eagle Valley for that reason..

Today, Carson City sits almost in the middle of Eagle Valley.

On January 17, 1854, the county of Carson was approved by the Governor and Legislative Assembly of the Territory of Utah, covering an area of over 20,000 square miles, including all of the inhabited portion of the western portion of the territory.

Through the vision of opportunist Abraham Curry and his partners, B.F. Green, J.J. Musser and Frank Proctor, Carson City was born in 1858.

Curry saw a thriving community, a prosperous town. He saw neatly laid out streets, lined with substantial homes. He saw a business center with a square in the middle. In that square there would be public buildings and a State Capitol.

Curry's dream got a significant boost when silver was discovered in the Comstock Lode. Carson City was the closest center for shipping and business exploded.

Carson City was on its way.

Early lithograph of Carson City, Utah Territory, 1858. Illustration first appeared in *Scenes of Wonder and Curiosity* from *Hutchings' California Magazine,* 1856-1861.

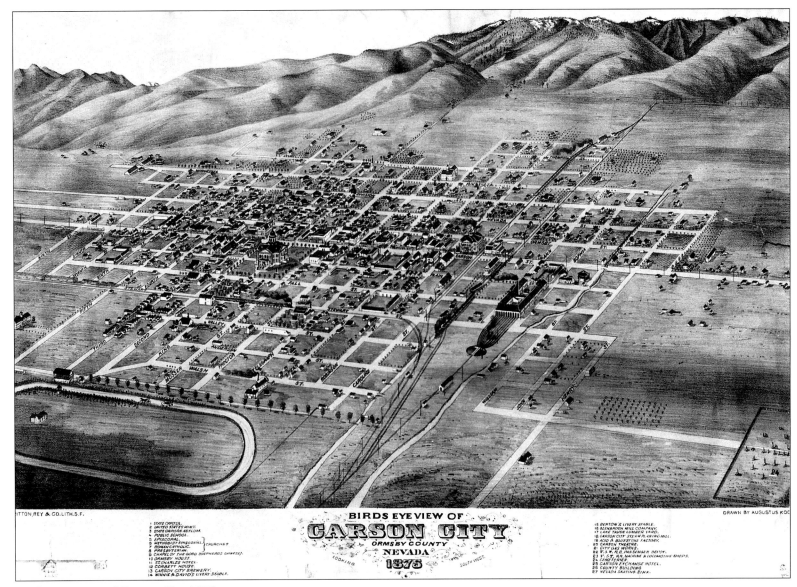

Bird's Eye View of Carson City, 1875.

William M. Stewart was a prominent mining lawyer and an influential member of the first territorial legislature representing Carson City. It was due to his political efforts that Carson City was named territorial capital in 1861. Stewart would later serve as Nevada's first U.S. Senator in 1864.

The first Territorial Legislature met on October 1, 1861 at Abe Curry's Warm Springs Hotel. Today, the Nevada State Prison occupies the site.

The hotel at Curry's Warm Springs was a popular resort for local settlers in the area.

James W. Nye (1814-1876). Nye was Territorial Governor of Nevada, 1861-1864 and United States Senator from, 1864-1872.

John Jacob Musser came to Carson County, Utah Territory in 1858 and was one of the founders of Carson City.

Carson City as it looked at the corner of Second and Carson streets in 1863.

Frank Proctor was one of the pioneers along with J.J. Musser, B.F. Green and Abe Curry who settled Carson City in 1858.

Major William Ormsby was an early Carson City pioneer who built the Ormsby House. He lost his life during the first battle of the Pyramid Lake Indian War in May, 1860.

Nevada Territorial Seal.

Abe Curry is one of the founders of Carson City in 1858. He was later superintendent of construction of the Carson City U.S. Mint and was also the first superintendent of the Mint. In addition, he built the Virginia and Truckee Railroad Enginehouse before his death in 1873.

THE NEW YORK HERALD.

WHOLE NO. 10,293.

NEW YORK WEDNESDAY, NOVEMBER 2, 1864.

PRICE FOUR CENTS.

RICHMOND.

Another Account of the Operations of the Second Corps in the Late Movements.

Attempt of the Rebels to Pierce Our Centre.

They are Driven Back with Heavy Loss,

THE SECOND CORPS.

THE NEW STATE OF NEVADA.

The Thirty-sixth Star in the Union--Its Latitude and Longitude.

THE NEW STATE OF NEVADA.

Description of the Commonwealth.

Its Riches in Gold, Silver, Rock Salt and Other Minerals.

A GREAT FIELD FOR EMIGRATION.

The Law Authorizing the State.

ANOTHER STAR FOR THE UNION,

GALLANT NAVAL EXPLOIT.

The Rebel Ram Albemarle Destroyed,

TERRIBLE RAILROAD CATASTROPHE

New York Herald, front page.

North Carson St. 1871
Carson City, Nev.

Carson City looking north from the top of the Capitol building in 1871.

Christopher "Kit" Carson had been trapping in the West for some 12 years when he first met John C. Fremont in 1842. The famous Indian fighter, hunter and scout served Fremont as guide on three expeditions (1842-1846). Fremont named the Carson River in honor of his trusted scout Kit Carson and later the founders of the community named the new town Carson City in 1858.

Mrs. William Ormsby was a prominent woman in Carson City in the early years. She appeared in this drawing wearing her Paris made ball gown which she wore to the Nevada Territorial Ball in October 1861. This dress is stored today at the Nevada State Museum's Russell Clothing and Textile Center in Carson City.

Schools & Education

According to Willa Oldham's book on Carson City, Ormsby County's potential school population in 1864 was reported to be 512 children between the ages of 4 and 21. Of those, 125 attended private schools and 173 attended the two public schools.

Teachers made anywhere from $40 to $125 per month at the time and had to pay a nickel for a teaching certificate.

The most famous Carson City school, according to Oldham's book, was the Sierra Seminary, a private school run by Hannah Clapp, Elizabeth Babcock and Mrs. E.H. Cutter.

Nevada was ahead of most areas in its concern for Indian education. For 90 years Stewart Indian School south of Carson City, was an institution for Indian education.

In 1887, the Nevada Legislature passed a bill creating "an Indian school for the purpose of training and educating Indian children." Land purchased was to be turned over to the federal government which agreed to operate the school. The first campus included 240 acres and on opening day in 1897, the school's enrollment was 37 students and three teachers.

Grade school students in front of the school at King and Division streets. (Frank Willis Day Collection)

Stewart Indian School students in a class on woodworking, ca. 1900.

Stewart Indian School students in front of administration building, ca. 1905.

Stewart Indian School, "Carson Indian Training Center," ca. 1900.

Stewart Indian School students work in the agricultural fields on school property.

Stewart Indian school male students dressed in uniforms in front of the administration building, ca. 1905. (Lucy Wright Collection, Walker River Paiute Tribal Archives, Schurz, Nevada)

Stewart Indian School
students learning
sewing, ca. 1900.

One of the many classrooms at the Stewart Indian School campus.

The Carson High School boys basketball team, 1920.

Pioneer educator Hannah Clapp and students at her Sierra Seminary school on Minnesota Street, ca. 1880.

The Carson High School, 1910.

Empire School during the 1890-1891 term. Percy King served as principal of the school.

Students of the North Ward School, ca. 1885.

Carson City School football team, ca. 1915.

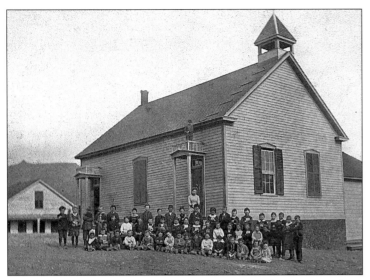

Students of South Ward School, ca. 1890. (Chester C. Sabins Collection)

The freshman class at Carson City High School in 1911. (Daun Bohall Collection)

The Central School located at Minnesota and Telegraph streets in 1875.

Government

When the split finally came that separated Nevada from Utah, Carson City became the territorial capitol in 1861.

That distinction didn't come without a battle. After all, most of the men attending the legislative session in 1861 were looking for an economic advantage for their own towns once statehood was achieved.

Fortunately, William M. Stewart, who had a law office in Carson City, fought harder than the rest. He also arranged for everyone who voted his way to get a county seat.

Today they might call that hardball politics.

On February 23, 1869, Governor Henry Goode Blasdel signed into law the "Capitol Building Bill." For somewhere in the neighborhood of $250, an architect was hired who drew up plans for a two-story building in the form of a Grecian cross. Specifications called for a building 148 feet in length and 98 feet in width.

It was ready by the time the Fifth Legislature convened in 1871.

Until 1969, when consolidation was approved, Carson City was the county seat for Ormsby County.

Major William Ormsby was a businessman and one of the area's earliest settlers. He was killed at the time of the first Indian encounter in the Pyramid Lake Indian War of 1860.

Lincoln County Assemblyman Levi Syphus studies an upcoming bill at his legislative desk in the Nevada Assembly in 1903.

The newly completed Nevada State Capitol in 1875. This photo was taken by Arnold Friend from across the street at the Ormsby House. (Dr. S.L. Lee Collection)

The Nevada State Capitol after the grounds had been landscaped and the iron fence erected. Photograph taken by Charlton E. Watkins, ca. 1877. An original print of this photograph is on display at the Nevada State Library and Archives.

The iron fence put up by Hannah Clapp back in 1875 as it appeared, ca. 1900.

Winter scene of the State Capitol building, ca. 1890.

Nevada State Capitol treeline front during the 1930s.

The capitol grounds early in the 1900s. In the distance is the bandstand used for summer concerts.

Nevada State Capitol building after the two wings were added in 1914 for additional space.

The Annex building was completed in 1906. Its west wall was only 25 feet from the State Capitol. The Nevada State Library remained in the annex until it outgrew it in 1936. Since then a number of state agencies have occupied the space,

The Office of the Surveyor General. The Surveyor General, Charles L. Deady, standing in the rear. Miss Bertha Sadler, clerk is at the right. Charles Deady, a member of the Silver-Democratic Party, was appointed February 25, 1908. He won the next election and served as Surveyor General until 1927.

The interior of the Nevada Assembly in 1939. The Lincoln portrait can be seen above the front dais.

Members of the Nevada State Senate standing in front of the Capitol building in 1897.

Adjutant General at his desk in the State Capitol, 1895.

State Land Office in the State Capitol, 1895.

The Supreme Court of Nevada sits for a portrait, ca. 1908. On the bench (left to right) are: Justices Frank H. Norcross, George F. Talbot and James F. Sweeney.

The Nevada State Controllers Office located on the first floor of the Capitol at the southeast corner. Sam P. Davis, Controller, standing at left. Davis, a member of the Silver-Democratic Party, served as Controller from 1899-1906. This photo was taken June 13, 1900.

State Printing staff, 1899. Seated in the photo are Andrew Maute, state printer, Will Mackey, foreman, Alf Daten, job printer, and George Maute, job printer. (Frances Humphrey Collection)

The old Armory building at Second and Fall Street, ca. 1905.

State Printing office, ca. 1900. (Noreen Humphreys Collection)

Nevada State Seal.

The Nevada State Senate turn to pose for the camera in 1911.

U.S. Post Office, ca. 1927. When it was completed in 1891 the Post Office was the first Federal office building in the State of Nevada. (Daun Bohall Collection)

Interior of the U.S. Post Office, ca, 1905. (Elliot Photograph)

Interior of the U.S.Post Office, ca. 1900.

The foundation of the U.S. Post Office being excavated in 1888.

Carson City U.S.
Mint, ca. 1875.

In the 1930s a man paid the U.S. Government $600 for the sole right to placer mine the dirt surrounding the Old Carson U.S. Mint building. He had about six months work and averaged $300 a month.

Architectural illustration of the Carson City U.S. Mint, ca. 1865. A.B. Mullett, Architect.

Cashier's Office at the Carson City U.S. Mint, 1895.

Superintendent of Public instruction H.C. Cuttings working at his desk in the State Capitol, 1895. He served from 1895-1898.

Deposit Melting Room, Carson City U.S. Mint, ca. 1870.

First coin press at the Carson City U.S. Mint, ca. 1870.

Carson City Mint employees in front of the building, ca. 1885. (Courtesy: National Archives)

Postcard of the interior of the State Prison yard, ca. 1910.

View of the entrance gate of the Nevada State Prison, ca. 1900.

Exterior wall of the Nevada State Prison, 1868.

Nevada State Prison, ca. 1875.

Boxing match taking place in the Nevada State Prison yard, 1916. (Renear Photograph)

Interior view of the prison yard, ca. 1916.

Nevada State Prison execution chamber. Nevada was the first state to use poison gas to execute convicted murderers. The first execution took place in 1924 when Gee Jon was executed with the use of gas. (Paul Carrington Collection)

Ormsby County Poor Farm at Clear Creek. Three and a half miles southwest of Carson City in Clear Creek Canyon. Superintendent Abrahams is standing on the porch, and Mrs. Abrahams is in the yard.

Judge Thomas P. Hawley at his desk in the U.S. Post Office building, ca. 1895. Judge Hawley was the first United States District Judge to preside in the new building.

Federal Court Room on the second floor of the U.S. Post Office building, ca. 1895. Judge Thomas P. Hawley is seated at the bench.

The Ormsby County Courthouse was designed by Nevada Architect Frederic J. DeLongchamps and built in 1920.

MANSION SITE DECIDED UPON

AND WILL BE LOCATED ON GROUND DONATED TO THE STATE BY HON. T. B. RICKEY

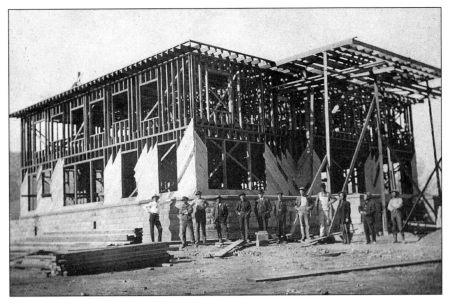

The Governor's Mansion under construction in 1909. (Burd Lindsay Collection)

Governor's Mansion, ca. 1915. When Tasker L. Oddie took office in 1911, he had the mansion painted completely white.

Postcard of the newly completed governor's mansion in August, 1910. Note the mansion is painted yellow (dark color) trimmed with white.

Governor Emmett D. Boyle of Nevada signing the resolution for ratification of the Nineteenth Amendment to the Constitution of the United States. Also pictured are: Mrs. Sadie D. Hurst who presented the resolution, Speaker of the Assembly D.J. Fitzgerald and a group of suffrage women, February 7, 1920.

V&T Railroad

In 1865 a charter was granted to the Virginia and Truckee Railroad Company. On September 19, 1872, regular train service began between Virginia City and Reno, via Carson City.

Service between Carson City and Reno continued until 1950.

Of all the buildings needed to house the various operations of the V&T, nothing was said to have compared with the erection of the engine house and machine shop in the middle of town.

An estimated 10 runs per day were made between Virginia City and Carson City. Many of the passengers were not just interested in the ore being moved to the quartz mills. The opera house in Virginia City was billing famous singers, actors and performers from around the world and the V&T took them to the shows in style.

The famous train line is today very much a part of Carson City's heritage and efforts to reopen the line continue.

V & T locomotive #22 Inyo being test steamed prior to shipment to Hollywood in 1937. This engine is now at the Nevada State Railroad Museum.

Carson City engine house and shops in the 1880s. Carson & Colorado locomotive tender on the transfer car at left.

V & T shop in 1882. Photographed by C.E. Peterson.

Train time at the Carson City station, in the ca. 1915.

Newly constructed V & T Station and general office in Carson City in 1872. Building was later lengthened, and is the Masonic Hall today.

V & T Carson City freight house on the site of the current post office.

A stock train coming into Carson City from Minden in 1937. (Ted Wurm Collection)

The V & T continued to use old fashioned stubbed switches until the end.(Guy Dunscomb Collection)

V & T Locomotive #11 Reno with the Lightning Express at the Carson City station, ca.1876.

The winter of January, 1916. Four locomotives bring the passenger train into Carson City at last, ending the snow blockade.

The snow plow train was not always the safest of duties. V & T locomotive #18 in trouble in January, 1890.

V & T locomotive #18 Dayton in winter snow plow duty.

Fancy interior of the V & T coach #18 as it appeared in 1938. (Daun Bohall Collection)

V & T excursion train coming down Washington Street to the depot in June, 1938. Photo by Ted Wurm. (Ted Wurm Collection)

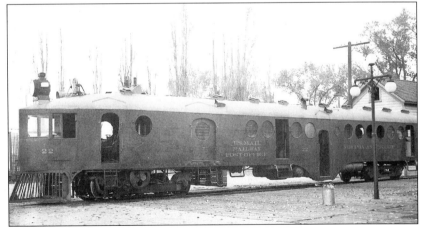

McKeen Motor Car #22 modernized passenger travel when it arrived in 1910. Seen here at the Carson City station platform in 1937 on its daily run. (Daun Bohall Collection)

V & T engine #25 taking up rails from Moundhouse in 1941, the end of the original Virginia City line.

Scene on the station platform in the 1890s. (Daun Bohall Collection)

V & T locomotive #1 Lyon behind the V & T shops in the late 1880s.

The arrival of Dan Stuart at the Carson City depot in March, 1897, for the Corbett - Fitzsimmons boxing match in which Fitzsimmons won the heavyweight title. Stuart had worked with Nevada officials to get a new law passed to allow boxing matches in February of 1897.

Grover Russell loading V & T Motor Car #99, preparing to make one of its last runs to Virginia City in June, 1938.

It took a lot of wood to fuel the old locomotives. V & T locomotives #20 and #24 at the wood lot.

The V & T continued to use old fashioned stubbed switches until the end. View looking east, ca. 1949. (Guy Dunscomb Collection)

Officials of the Virginia &Truckee Railroad. General Manager H.M. Yerington seated in the center. (Daun Bohall Collection)

Shop workers of the Virginia and Truckee Railroad posed next to the depot, ca. 1907. (Daun Bohall Collection)

Interior of the V & T machine shop in the late 1800s. (Daun Bohall Collection)

Pouring iron in the V & T foundry for the last time in 1935. (Daun Bohall Collection)

V & T shops blacksmith shop.

The V & T shops also did outside work. Name plate from the Carson City U.S. Mint coin press number 1.

A road grader built in the V & T shops. (Daun Bohall Collection)

Repairing V & T coach #4 in the carpentry shop. (Daun Bohall Collection)

Business & Downtown

It was wealth that brought most early settlers to Carson City. There was silver and gold in the hills and opportunities abounded for visionaries who saw the endless possibilities.

Hordes of prospectors came to Carson City for shipping and supplies.

Before he was killed in the Paiute uprising, Major Ormsby built a hotel hoping to attract lawmakers once the new territory was organized. The Ormsby House lives on today, a testimony to Carson City's resilient character.

And the exploding timber industry, needed to supply the mines of Virginia City, brought hundreds of workers to Carson City.

As it does today, gambling provided much of the entertainment as miners with full pockets looked to increase their fortunes at the poker tables.

Provisions were scarce in Carson City and the prices high. Flour went for as much as 60 cents a pound, sugar a dollar a pound, and hay for $350 a ton. Freight wagons ran through Carson City in an endless stream. On August 17, 1866, the *Appeal* reported "about twenty-five teams passed through Carson City on their way to Virginia City yesterday."

Interior of the Frank Willis Day Dry good store, ca. 1885. Frank Day is seated to the left of his employees standing behind the counter. (Frank Willis Day Collection)

Carson City residents crossing Carson Street on their way to the Carson City Mint, ca. 1895. The Virginia and Truckee Railroad passenger train has just arrived at the Carson City Depot. (Daun Bohall Collection)

The Park Hotel, which was formerly the Ormsby House, decorated for the 4th of July, ca. 1900. A group of men standing outside of the hotel waiting for the parade to begin down Carson Street. (Daun Bohall Collection)

South Carson Street looking north in 1893. The two-story building to the left is the St. Charles Hotel.

View looking West up King Street from the top of the State Capitol, ca. 1895. (Daun Bohall Collection)

View of Carson Street in 1877. This illustration appeared in *Out West On The Overland Train: Across-the-Continent Excursion with Leslie's Magazine* in 1877.

A buggy moving south down Carson Street in front of the Arlington Hotel, ca.1890. The Carson City U.S. Mint is located just to the north of the Arlington Hotel.

Carson City citizens posing for this photograph in front of the Gray Reid Wright building, the Arlington Hotel and Carson City U.S. Mint Building, ca. 1900. (Daun Bohall Collection)

The St. Charles Hotel served as the main stage stop in Carson City, ca. 1875. The St. Charles was one of the most elegant hotels in the state.

The Sweeney building located at the corner of King and Curry streets was one of the earliest commercial buildings in Carson City. It was built in 1860. The building to the west was owned by Sweeney's son-in-law Peter Cavanaugh, who operated a bakery and cracker factory. Cavanaugh was awarded the contract and built the Nevada State Capitol building in 1870-1871.

Carson Opera House shortly before it burned in the late 1930s.

The business block of Mrs. M.E. Rinckel, ca. 1881. (Daun Bohall Collection)

The Bullion and Exchange Bank building - located at the corner of Carson and Proctor - was built in 1876. (Daun Bohall Collection)

The Ormsby House on the southwest corner of Carson and Second streets, ca. 1890. (Daun Bohall Collection)

The Capitol House, a popular boarding house, being relocated as it passes by the State Capitol building, ca. 1910. (Daun Bohall Collection)

The Circe Hotel was located on the corner of West Caroline and North Carson streets across from the Carson City U.S. Mint building ca. 1895.(Daun Bohall Collection)

Winter scene at the corner of Musser and Carson streets in 1916. Meyers Hardware, Kitzmeyer's Drug Store and the Emporium are the businesses that occupied the west side of Carson Street. (Daun Bohall Collection)

Carson Street looking north during the fall of 1876. The political banner across the street is in support of the Republican national ticket of Hayes - Wheeler, Photograph by Charleton E. Watkins.

Business ad for the *Carson Daily Appeal,* 1869. The *Appeal* was first published May 16, 1865 and was a morning paper with only four pages. The Appeal was located in Boyd's brick building on Second Street, across from the State Capitol building.

Ida May Bohall standing behind the counter in the American Tea Store, ca. 1918. The store was located at 104 South Carson Street. (Daun Bohall Collection)

The interior of Meyer's Hardware store at the corner of Musser and Carson streets, ca. 1900. (Daun Bohall Collection)

Nevada State Children's Home, ca. 1910.

Nevada State Children's Home, ca. 1917.

The Nevada State Orphan's Home was authorized in 1869 by the Nevada State Legislature and a building was constructed in Carson to house the state's orphans. The first child was admitted October 28, 1870. This photo shows the State Orphan's Home, ca. 1885. (Adrian Atwater Collection)

Children from the state children home, ca. 1910. The children's home was also called Sunny Acres by local residents.

Carson Street looking south in 1897. The Carson City U.S. Mint is located on the right side of the street.(Daun Bohall Collection)

Automobiles parked in front of the Capitol building, ca. 1938.

Carson Street looking south, ca. 1934. (Daun Bohall Collection)

Carson Street looking north, ca. 1925. (Daun Bohall Collection)

The North End Livery and Feed Stable owned by D. Circe, ca. 1895. (Daun Bohall Collection)

Benton's Livery Stable. J. M. "Doc" Benton in the spring of 1864 came across the plains to Nevada, and was engaged in mining and milling until 1867 when he entered the livery and stable business in Carson City. His stable was located on the northeast corner of Carson and Third streets. He also was the proprietor of the stage line running between Carson and Lake Tahoe. "Doc" Benton in the buggy. (Daun Bohall Collection)

State Capitol building looking east on King Street, ca. 1900.

Carson Street business fronts across from the State Capitol grounds, ca. 1905. The streets were sprinkled regularly to hold down the dust. (Daun Bohall Collection)

Automobile traveling down tree-lined King Street towards the State Capitol, ca. 1925.

William Harris Sweetland Cobbler Shop on the northeast corner of Carson and Proctor streets. The building was remodeled into the Brick Sweetland building in 1938. (Daun Bohall Collection)

Carson City flying service hanger at the airport, ca. 1938.

Roventini and Bartlett Garage on Carson Street, ca. 1940. (Daun Bohall collection)

The popular Senator Cafe and Casino on Carson Street in the late 1930s. (Daun Bohall Collection)

Dutch Mill food stand located at the intersection of US 50 and Carson Street, ca. 1936. (Daun Bohall Collection)

Interior of F.J. Steinmetz City Drug Store on August 3, 1899. Steinmetz on left and Jacob Muller on the right. The Store located on West Carson Street between Telegraph and Spear streets. (Daun Bohall Collection)

Downtown Carson City looking north on Carson Street, ca. 1930. (Daun Bohall Collection)

Residential

Many of Carson City's grand homes still stand today, thanks to historical preservation efforts and immense community pride.

There's the D.L. Bliss mansion, for example. Bliss owned a quarter interest in some 7,000 acres of timber in the Lake Tahoe area and built his home on West Robinson Street of Tahoe sugar pine and cedar.

Not far from the Bliss home lived Dr. W. H. Cavell, who in 1907 imported an architect from Oakland to provide modern touches, including hot water.

Dr. S. L. Lee and H.H. Springmeyer were neighbors on North Minnesota Street. The 11-room Lee home was built in 1906 on the site of a former Carson City school. Springmeyer's home later became home to Governor Charles H. Russell.

Carson City merchant Hyman Olcovich built his beautiful home on North Curry Street in 1876. His home was the center of controversy in 1997 as Carson City sought to move it in an effort to pave the way for more parking downtown. As this book was published, historians were attempting to save the home.

The D.A. Bender home at 707 West Robinson Street. Pictured here are some of the graduates of Carson High School, August 29, 1896.

The T.B. Rickey Home at 512 North Mountain Street.

Carson City residence, ca. 1885.

The Rinckel Mansion located at 102 North Curry Street, ca. 1938. Mathias "Matt" Rinckel built the mansion in 1875-1876.

The Thorne Ranch house, ca. 1890.

The Bliss Mansion was built by Duane L. Bliss, lumber and railroad magnate, in 1879. When completed, this home was the most modern and largest home in Nevada. It was the first home in Nevada entirely piped for gas lighting.

The residents of the home at the northwest corner of Robinson and Curry pose outside for the photographer, ca. 1880. (Daun Bohall Collection)

Benard Supera's home located on the corner of Curry and Washington streets, ca. 1885. (Daun Bohall Collection)

The Bath family home, ca. 1890. (Adrian Atwater Collection)

Interior of the parlor of Judge Charles H. Belknap home in Carson City, ca. 1900.

Carson City residence, ca. 1890. (Adrian Atwater Collection)

Nevada Supreme Court Justice Charles Henry Belknap and wife Virginia in their front yard at 1206 North Nevada Street, ca. 1897. The home was originally built in 1875 by Oscar T. Barber. He sold the home to Justice Belknap in 1881.

Frank Murphy home located at 1112 North Carson Street in the 1930s. Murphy worked for the Virginia and Truckee Railroad as general manager. (Daun Bohall Collection)

Abe Curry home at 406 North Nevada Street. This house was built in 1871 of sandstone quarried from the Nevada State Prison.

This home was originally built by William Stewart in 1860. He later sold it to Territorial Governor James W. Nye in 1862. At the time of this drawing in 1881 it was owned by Mrs. H. Shrieves.

The Roberts home, ca. 1873. House built by James D. Roberts in Washoe City in 1859 and then moved to Carson City in 1873 on a V & T flat car.

Carson City residence located on North Curry Street, ca. 1880. (Daun Bohall Collection)

Judge Michael A. Murphy and family in the front yard of their home at 1112 North Carson Street, ca. 1897. (Jay C. Robinson Collection)

Baldy home on Walsh Street. This house was built by O'Brien of the Mackay, Fair, Flood and O'Brien fame. The house was moved to Carson City and owned by Elmer Baldy. In 1932 the home was again moved this time to Gardnerville, Nevada. (Daun Bohall Collection)

The E.P. Esser home located at 306 South Minnesota Street was designed by Esser's brother-in-law John Conant and built in 1907. An identical home would be constructed the same year by the Cavells on Robinson Street. The Essers were upset when they learned that the Cavells had purchased the same house plans as theirs. (Frances Humphrey Collection)

Residences of Charles F. Bicknell and George C. Thaxter in 1881.

The home of Carson City clothier Frank Willis Day, ca. 1895. (Frank Willis Day Collection)

The home of Governor and Mrs. Jewett Adams. The home was later purchased by State Printer Andrew Maute and his family. This photo was taken around 1900. (Frances Humphrey Collection)

Mexican Mill Superintendent home located in Empire, ca. 1888. (Daun Bohall Collection)

Interior view of the front parlor of the Rinckel Mansion built in 1876. Rinckel and his wife imported many of the furnishings, custom-made lace curtains and chandeliers from France.

Industry

While Carson City is home today for manufacturers who supply NASA with spaceship parts, the city's early days saw timber, silver and railroad barons. Carson City was said to resemble one huge lumber yard, with thousands of cords of wood piled to the skies.

Sawmills flourished. Some used steam-powered equipment to turn out as much as 15,000 feet of lumber in a single day.

Meanwhile, the frantic search for gold and silver continued. In 1868, there were an estimated 33 silver mills from Virginia City to Seven Mile Canyon, Gold Hill and American Flat.

By the spring of 1860 freight lines were employing 2,000 men and using 12,000 to 15,000 mule and horses to carry the ore from Virginia City to California.

Eureka mill dam, Brunswick Canyon, 1889. Photograph by J. H. Crockwell.

Eureka Mill on the Carson River near Empire, 1889. Photograph by J. H. Crockwell.

Eureka Cyanide Plant Mill along the Carson River.

Eureka Mill dam on the Carson River, 1889. Photograph by J.H. Crockwell.

Eureka mill on the Carson River near Empire, 1889. Photograph taken by J.H. Crockwell.

Merrimac Mill on the Carson River, ca. 1877. Photograph by Charlton E. Watkins.

Brunswick Mill along the Carson River, ca. 1877. Photograph by Charlton E. Watkins.

Brunswick Mill on the Carson River.

Upper End of Carson & Tahoe Lumber and Flume Co. Lumber & Wood Yard near Carson City, ca. 1877. Photograph by Charlton E. Watkins.

Carson & Tahoe Lumber and Flume Company transfer yard and flume at Spooner Summit, ca. 1877. Photograph by Charlton E. Watkins.

V-Flume from Spooner down Clear Creek Canyon to Carson City and the V&T Railroad, ca. 1890.

Lumber yards, flumes and Virginia and Truckee Railroad one mile south of Carson City, ca. 1877. Photograph by Charlton E. Watkins.

Carson and Tahoe Lumber and Fluming Company railroad train moving lumber from Glenbrook to Spooner to be flumed down to Carson City, ca. 1877. Photograph taken by Charlton E. Watkins.

Mexican Dam along the Carson River, ca. 1886. (Daun Bohall Collection) Note the men fishing from the dam.

V-Flume in Clear Creek Canyon, 1893.

Freight wagon leaving Carson City for the mining town of Bodie in 1892. (Daun Bohall Collection)

Horse team moving hay on a flatbed wagon passing through Carson City. (Daun Bohall Collection)

Nevada's first brewery was Wagner & Kleins Carson City Brewery in 1860. By 1865, a new two-story brewery building was completed. The first floor was used for brewing purposes and storage.

Carson Brewing Company building in the late 1930s. The building was later used by the *Nevada Appeal*.

Carson Box factory, 1893. This is the site of Copeland Lumber Company today. (Daun Bohall Collection)

Thorne Ranch, ca. 1890s.

The brick yard in Carson City, ca. 1880.

Horse drawn buggy crossed V-Flume in Clear Creek Canyon. (Frances Humphrey Collection)

Carson River wood drive, 1888. Photograph by Carson City photographer C.E. Peterson.

Wood drive on the Carson River, 1888. Photograph by C.E. Peterson.

V-Flume Clear Creek Canyon, 1893. (Frances Humphrey collection)

Carson River Wood Drive, 1888. Photograph taken by Carson City photographer C.E. Peterson.

Aaron D. Treadway ranch and resort was a popular spot for social activities in the 1800s. This illustration comes from Thompson's and West *History of Nevada*, 1881.

People & Society

One of the more famous residents of Carson City was Samuel Clemens, otherwise known as Mark Twain. As a reporter for the *Territorial Enterprise* he spent a good deal of his time in Carson City with his brother, Orion Clemens, who became Territorial Secretary and sometime acting governor.

Before the frontier journalist ever penned his first adjectives about Carson City, other well-known pioneers had already blazed their paths.

Among them were Lieutenant John C. Fremont and his most trusted aide Christopher "Kit" Carson. In 1843, Fremont led his men on an exploration of the Carson River basin on their way across the Sierra Nevada Mountains to the Sacramento Valley.

And Carson City has had its share of leaders and characters over her many years.

There was Hank Monk, prince of the stagecoach drivers. He rode for Wells Fargo over the dangerous roads between Sacramento and Virginia City wearing his trademark battered hat and trousers stained with tobacco juice. Monk was rumored to feed his horses whiskey to make them run faster.

Native Americans were and still are a large part of Carson City's heritage. The Washoe Indians were basket makers. So perfect were their baskets that they were once used as a medium of exchange.

Gentleman Jim Corbett and Bob Fitzsimmons fought for the world heavyweight boxing championship in 1897 on St. Patrick's Day. The fight lasted 14 rounds, ending in a knockout for Fitzsimmons.

Carson City band at Cooke's Grove, May 25, 1890. (Daun Bohall Collection)

Pioneer businessman E.B. Rail came to Carson City in 1861 and operated a hardware store. His store was located on the west side of Carson Street between Fourth and Fifth streets.

Carson City Capitol Grange meeting after a buggy ride, ca. 1890. (Noreen Humphreys Collection)

A group of Carson City residents photographed outside a tent at the Ormsby County Fair, October 4, 1895. (Courtesy: Bud Klette)

The Carson City Wheelmen, ca. 1895.

Dr. William Cavell and friends going on a bicycle ride, ca. 1910. (Noreen Humphreys Collection)

Carson City pioneer educator Hannah Hezekiah Clapp, ca. 1885. Hannah founded the Sierra Seminary in Carson in the 1860s. She was also the contractor who built the iron fence that still stands around the State Capitol.

Mathias "Matt" Rinckel settled in Carson City in 1863 and operated a butcher shop called the Eagle Market. He was a successful businessman and in 1875 began construction of a mansion which was finished in 1876. He was to enjoy the home for only three years before his death in 1879, at the age of 43.

Carson City band, 1867.

Carson, City Warren Engine Company fighting a fire downtown, ca. 1900.

The Nevada State Band was organized in Carson City in September, 1896. They held concerts during the summer and fall at the bandstand on the State Capitol lawn.

Burning of Joe Kelly's stock of liquor and tobacco at the corner of Fourth and Carson streets. The Reverend Yorkum, a preacher passing through Carson City led this event on December 20, 1909. (Daun Bohall Collection)

St. Peter's Episcopal Church and Rectory, ca. 1900. The first service was held in the church August 9, 1868. It cost $5,500 to build. (Noreen Humphreys Collection)

First Presbyterian Church, ca. 1905. The church was completed in 1864 and it is considered the oldest church building still standing in service in Nevada.

St. Teresa of Avila Catholic Church, ca. 1938. Built originally in 1870-1871 of wood frame, it is presently faced with brick. (Daun Bohall Collection)

First Methodist Church, ca. 1900. The congregation was organized in 1859 and completed the church in 1867. Reverend Warren Nims, the pastor of the church from 1863 to 1866, was responsible for much of the construction including hauling the stone from the State Prison quarry. The church was dedicated on the 8th of September, 1867 and cost $10,000 to build. The congregation is the oldest of its denomination in the state, and the church is known as "The Cradle of Nevada Methodism." (Noreen Humphreys Collection)

Pioneer physician and surgeon Simeon Lemuel Lee, (1844-1927). He served as Surgeon General of Nevada, with the rank of colonel. Dr. Lee was also an avid collector and collected stamps, arrowheads, baskets, stones, minerals, ceramics, fossils, guns, and other rare objects. Dr. Lee's collection was given to the State of Nevada in 1934.

Charles W. Friend's observatory and weather station on the corner of East King and Stewart streets. Charles Friend is considered Nevada's First Weatherman for his pioneer efforts to organize our state's weather system in the late 1800s.

Eve Eugenia Stone on her favorite horse Joe Breckenridge, ca. 1897.

Charles W. Friend inside of his observatory preparing to look through his six-inch equatorial telescope. Friend received international recognition by the Royal Geographical Society in London for discovering an unknown comet in the 1870s.

Governor John Sparks seated in his office at the State Capitol, ca. 1905. Governor Sparks, known as "Honest John Sparks," was a cattleman his entire life. Sparks also signed the legislation for the construction of the Governor's Mansion in 1907.

Dr. William Cavell takes his family and friends for a Sunday ride along the Carson River, ca. 1910. (Noreen Humphreys Collection)

Maude Stern Mortensen hunting in the Sierra Nevada mountains, ca, 1900. (Frances Humphrey Collection)

Billy Lynch was Abe Lincoln's confidential messenger and body servant and witnessed the assassination of President Lincoln. After the assassination, Billy worked for President Andrew Johnson until 1868. Abe Curry befriended him during a visit to Washington, D.C. and brought him to Carson City where he worked as porter at the Carson City U.S. Mint. (Daun Bohall Collection)

Datsolalee is considered one of the finest Native American basket makers in the United States. Gathering willow, fern, and birch with the aid of her husband, she wove into her masterpieces the legends of her people "The Washoe" and their love of nature. Her baskets are unsurpassed for artistic conception and symbolic importance. Her baskets are found in museums throughout America, and the Nevada State Museum in Carson City has an exhibit of her work.

Abe Cohn is shown proudly displaying two of Datsolalee degikup baskets behind the Emporium. He served as her agent and kept records of her work and sold them from his store. The Emporium was a museum of Indian art and handicraft, as well as a marketplace.

Henry M. "Hank" Monk (1829-1883) famous stagecoach driver, ca. 1870. Hank drove the Carson City-Lake Tahoe section of the overland mail stage route.

The Hank Monk Schottische was composed by local Carson City resident J.P. Meder to commemorate the famous stage ride taken by New York newspaper editor Horace ("Go West, young man") Greeley from Carson City to Placerville, California with Monk driving the stage.

Dr, Anton W. Tjader was a pioneer physician in Carson City. He was born in St. Petersburg, Russia in 1825 and served in the Russian Army during the Crimean War of 1854. Dr. Tjader emigrated to the United States in 1855 and reached Genoa in September, 1859, where he set up a medical practice. He moved his practice to Carson City in 1860 and remained there until his death on July 8, 1870.

Carson City had a large chinese population. Carson City herb doctor Wai Tong used Chinese herbs and medicine to treat the ills of the Chinese and other residents throughout the area. (Frances Humphrey Collection)

Hattie Humphrey preparing to send a telegraph message from her telegraph office located on Carson Street, ca. 1890. (Noreen Humphreys Collection)

Recreation & Celebration

Parades still march down Carson Street, just as they have for the past 100 years or so.

Nevadans have a reputation as a hard-working breed. So, too, are they known for their abilities to enjoy life.

With its near perfect climate, Carson City and its neighboring environs are attractive for the outdoor recreationists.

Hiking, horseback riding, fishing, hunting, boating and biking were as popular in the early days of Carson City as they are today.

Tree-lined streets were inviting for Sunday strolls and lush city parks were perfect settings for a picnic.

In the evening there was opera and the opera house and always some good conversation to be found in one of many saloons.

Admission Day parade passing in front of the Ormsby County Courthouse in 1938. "Swede" Nelson entertains the crowd on his high-wheeled bicycle. Photograph by Ernie Mack.

President Theodore Roosevelt was welcomed to the Nevada State Capitol as the Hero of San Juan Hill in 1903.

President Theodore Roosevelt addressing the large crowd in front of the Capitol on May 19, 1903. The President's podium stood on the front steps beneath an arch of army muskets, and bayonets, and was flanked by two buffalo heads. His chair was made of elk horns.

The United States Post Office building is decorated to honor President Roosevelt as he passed on his way to the Capitol, May 19, 1903. (Daun Bohall Collection)

The crowd begins to gather to hear President Roosevelt address them from the front steps of the Capitol in 1903. (Daun Bohall Collection)

Banners and flags were strewn across Carson Street as President Roosevelt's carriage made its way to the Capitol building in 1903.

The University of Nevada President Dr. J.E. Stubbs addressing the crowd gathered in front of the State Capitol building on the 4th of July in 1895.

Carson City residents gather at the corner of Carson and Musser streets and wait for the 4th of July parade to pass. The Ormsby County building is decorated with banners and U.S. flags for the special city celebration.

Carson City ladies enjoy going for a summer automobile ride, ca. 1925. (Frances Humphrey Collection)

Ormsby County Fair poster, 1892. County fairs attracted large crowds and harness racing was one of the most popular events held each year. This unique poster is presently on display at the Nevada State Museum.

The Cavell and Platt families having a picnic along the Carson River, ca. 1910. (Noreen Humphreys Collection)

The pioneer clothing merchant Joseph Platt and family shown enjoying a special family time together, ca. 1910. (Noreen Humphreys Collection)

A group of local Carson City musicians preparing to give a concert, ca. 1897. (Frank Willis Day Collection)

World Champion Gentleman Jim Corbett posing before his championship match with Bob Fitzsimmons on March 17, 1897.

James Corbett and his wife inspect the ring and fight site before the championship fight on March 17, 1897. The world's attention was focused on Carson City that day, and challenger Bob Fitzsimmons defeated the champion in the 14th round to take the title.

Acting Governor Reinhold Sadler used this ticket to attend the fight. (Nevada State Museum Collection)

Arrival of World Champion James J. Corbett and his brother Harry at the Virginia and Truckee Railroad station in Carson City. The drawing appeared in the *San Francisco Examiner.*

Corbett and Fitzsimmons World Heavy Weight Championship Fight took place on St. Patrick Day, March 17, 1897. Fitzsimmons won the fight in the 14th round with a knockout of the champion Corbett. This was the first heavyweight fight to be filmed and eventually netted the promoter about a million dollars.

The Knights of Templer parade down Carson Street towards the Capitol, ca. 1895.

The 4th of July parade coming down Musser street turned south onto Carson Street to pass in front of the State Capitol in 1892.

The Animal Alliance Fountain, across from the State Capitol, ca. 1915. The fountain was designed specifically to meet the needs of Carson City's four-legged residents.

A patriotic entry passes in front of the State Capitol during the July 4, 1914 parade. (Daun Bohall Collection)

Nevada Governor Emmett Derby Boyle proudly greets the commander of the U.S. Army Lincoln Highway expedition in front of the State Capitol in August, 1919. The expedition traveled over many miles of primitive roads to prove that troops could be moved across the country from Washington, D.C. to San Francisco.

Carson City residents enjoying a dance and social event at the Armory Hall, ca. 1893. The Armory Hall was located on the east side of Carson Street between East Ann and East Washington streets.

Admission Day parade, 1939.

Crowds gather to watch the Admission Day parade in front of the Ormsby County Courthouse in 1940. (Daun Bohall Collection)

Carson City Admission Day float entry celebrating 81 years of statehood.

The Admission Day parade depicts an old time tea party as it passes by the Sprouse-Reitz Company store on Carson Street in 1938. Photo by Ernie Mack.

Opening day attracted large crowds on Nevada Day October 31, 1941 to see the new Nevada State Museum.

WPA workers on May 7, 1941 remodeling the old Carson City Mint building to prepare it to be used as the Nevada State Museum.

Carson City Street Fair button, July 3-8, 1901. (From the Nevada State Museum Collection)

Admission Day parade, October 31, 1939.

Carson City Sagebrush Club gather in Clear Creek Canyon for a picnic, ca. 1932.